AMERICAN TRUCKS

AMERICAN TRUCKS

A PHOTOGRAPHIC ESSAY OF AMERICAN TRUCKS AND TRUCKING

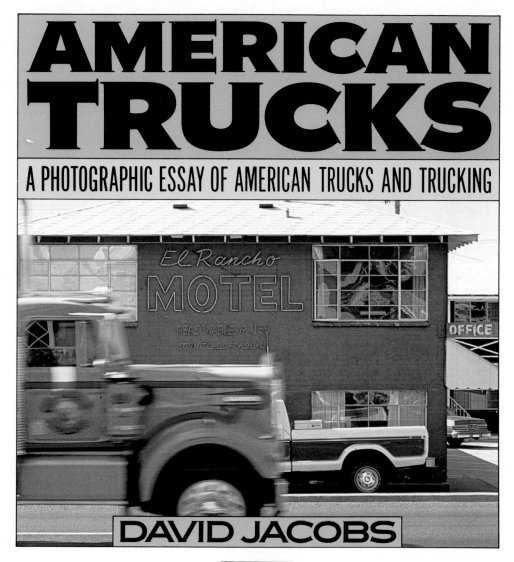

DAVID JACOBS

OSPREY

First published in winter 1980 by Osprey Publishing Limited
12-14 Long Acre, London WC2E 9LP
Member company of the George Philip Group
Reprinted winter 1981

British Library Cataloguing in Publication Data
Jacobs, David
American trucks.
1. Motor-trucks – North America – Pictorial works
I. Title
629.22'4'097   TL230
ISBN 0–85045–379–8

Editor Tim Parker
Printed in Hong Kong

The American truck and the life of the American truck driver have always been seen as romantic and free-moving, as latter day leftovers of the Wild West. At least, by the truck drivers themselves.
Their phenomena has become our's. Today, thousands of followers search for books, magazines, photographs, films and records on this 'tough guy's' way of life. What is a job of work to the truck driver together with the tools he uses, has become a passion for the truck enthusiast, world wide.
American Trucks is for those enthusiasts who may never see 'coast to coast' through the windshield of an eighteen wheeler, who may never hear the pounding of a conventional Pete or KW 'pouring on the coal' in its homeland, or the chatter of the ubiquitous CB radio as drivers pass the day. It's also for those who have, yet want to be constantly reminded. Here is a photographic essay, all in colour, to tempt you.

Photographer David Jacobs' self portrait

There isn't a greater truck buff than
photographer David Jacobs. His
work has captured with great feeling
the very heart of the American
trucker and his very special world.
This book is dedicated to all David's
truckin' friends including Lizzy,
Steve, Dave S, Gobbs, Ivor and
Naomi and especially to the many
hospitable truckers whom he has met
in the USA.

CONTENTS

ON THE MOVE

Left High speed and nose to tail. This is East Coast, near Lancaster in Ohio. GMC cabover pulling a refrigerated trailer, reefer or cold box, leads another cabover, a Ford

Arizona, a place called Williams, close to the Grand Canyon sees an old Peterbilt conventional, 6 wheeler tar truck in the early morning ready to start out

Freeway in the early evening. The San Diego ten lane freeway is thought to be the busiest highway in the world. Taken from a flyover on the freeway going north out of Los Angeles this Peterbilt conventional double tanker carrying gasoline is something over the speed limit
Right Tall, strong and fast. A Kenworth conventional tanker is passed on the road to Kingman in Arizona

Still not much different from the cowboy days, Williams in Arizona is a
typical busy 'trucking town' full of diners and motels. A thundering
Peterbilt conventional hauls its Thermo King on to Bakersfield

Out of Barstow in California is nearly ten miles of desert roller coaster – single lane but straight as a die. National fleet rental Lee Way White Freightliner cabover is really humming *Overleaf* Slowing down, down into the valley at Williams in Arizona, this immaculate KW (Kenworth) conventional shatters the peace of the countryside. Lots of chrome is in evidence as are the twin stacks and CB antennae

Cement powder in a double trailer in the setting
sun. Some ninety miles south of Flagstaff in
Arizona this Peterbilt drones its way home over a
flyover

Left International cabover with the Hoover Dam in the background on the way to Boulder City. Air temperature 115°F. *Right* The simple Kenworth emblem mounted on the over-built hinged flip-up cap

Well over the legal limit in the midday sun! No licence plates visible (they are on the side of the cab) but a lot of money spent on the rig. Winged bird on the radiator marks this KW as something special *Right, top* Old White Freightliner emblem. *Bottom* 'Bugs on the bumper' – this Peterbilt has travelled overnight through the Arizona desert and this is the inevitable result

This Peterbilt conventional has been built specially to enable it to take the tight corners in the area of the Hoover Dam, where it is photographed. The trailer is far from the cab probably because the cab is fitted with a sliding fifth wheel, or slider wheel

Left Chucking out lots of exhaust smoke this beer hauling Freightliner cabover climbs a steep gradient in the Hoover Dam area *Above* Out of Fresno, California this twin stack sleeper unit hauling fresh vegetables and fruit is at high speed. Actual speed estimates are difficult although under good conditions 85 plus mph is readily available

The Favorite Manufacturing company have chosen this very special Marmon to pull their trailer. The Texan built Marmon is rare, though the air conditioning unit and twin stacks and air horns make it stand out here close to Williams, in Arizona

Shot from fourteen floors up in a hotel block close to the freeway this beautiful Peterbilt merges its subtle red and chrome with its speed. High speed fuel on the San Diego freeway in Beverly Hills *Right* Ready mix on the upper level of the San Francisco Bay Bridge. Early morning mist

Peterbilt eighteen-wheeler with factory painted cabover. Nothing fancy for this East Coast rig

Downtown Manhattan, New York. These heavy trucks wreck the old cobbled streets. 'Big J' is probably hauling refuse and is seen close to Queensboro Bridge. This is not a long haul rig although the Peterbilt is equipped with CB radio

Beautiful sign writing is, of course, not uncommon. Nor is the tradition of the 'old' Wild West. Death Valley is close to Las Vegas – old Route 66 crosses it to the south

Left Close to Barstow again, on Route 15, an old double tanker Peterbilt conventional captured at very high speed. This rig is over ten years old but has proven itself to be supremely reliable over very high mileages *Above* Sunrise in Ventura close to Los Angeles city – smog or mist, or both?

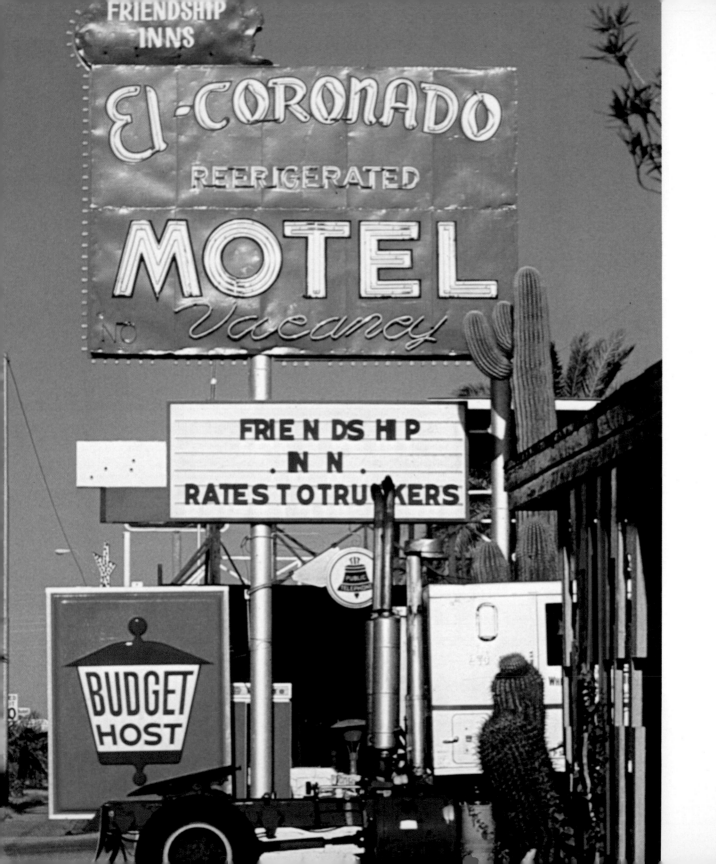

TRUCKSTOP

Left Gila Bend, Arizona and a sleeper cabover parked for the night. This is a typical
motel in the desert with its cactus and high temperature (95 °F at 6.00 am!). Most
rooms come for $8 per night with bed, television and noisy air conditioner thrown in.
The rig's trailer is parked elsewhere *Above* Drink Schlitz! Truckers are encouraged
to drink a great deal – Coke, Coors, Budweiser and Schlitz – being served iced water
even with coffee everywhere they go. This sign hangs in a typical diner *Overleaf* In the
midday heat a Continental Trailways coach hides behind this Kenworth
conventional having its engine oil checked. This rig was caught during a quick
stopover on Route 5 close to Los Banos in California, around sixty miles south of
Oakland

Left, top Gila Bend, Arizona, on the road side *Bottom* 'No shoes, no shirt, no service' and what looks like no customers too for this diner in the early evening in Yuma, California *Right* Unusual as a tractor pulling a reefer, GMC conventionals are more often seen as smaller straight jobs or bobtails

Barstow, California where the heat runs
higher than the price of gas 91.9 cents for a
US gallon of regular in this station

Top Apart from drinking truckers are also encouraged to eat and gamble. This Peterbilt double tanker gear jammer is passing by Boulder City close to Las Vegas *Bottom, left* Mounted on a Mack fire truck used by the San Clemente Fire Department *Right* This winged mascot completes the heavy custom on this conventional Pete *Overleaf* Around 100,000 US gallons of gas sits in these KW double tankers on an early Sunday morning in Oceanside, Southern California. Four of them are stopped in a closed gas station with their drivers visiting a diner

Below, left Almost a fish eye view in the back of one of the chromed tankers featured on the previous spread *Right* $36 a wash for the whole rig *Opposite* Rigs are washed partly by hand and partly by machine. Custom paintwork can only be shown off if its clean. Lots of truck stops have this facility

Left This double sleeper Peterbilt
conventional cold box runs east to west in
three days non-stop using two drivers. It's
photographed at Harrisburg, Pennsylvania
although it's based at St Louis and is one of
twelve rigs run by a father and son outfit
Above A white Freightliner ignores the sign
at Gila Bend in Arizona just after dawn

Furniture removals is big business because many Americans move house frequently. This rigid box van is fairly unusual because of its length. It was photographed outside a furniture store in Flagstaff, Arizona

Left, top A long way from home and a much more
common removal rig. This is a sleeper cabover in Baker
near Las Vegas *Bottom* Named after the truck in a
film this beautiful KW is run by an owner-operator.
During a union dispute this independent was shot at by a
sniper through his windshield *Above* San Diego,
Southern California. KW, Aerodyne and reefer outside
a motel

Hard on the brakes, change gear –
many, many times for this GMC
sleeper cabover as it travels close to
the Hoover Dam around the many
hairpin bends. Again this one is far
from home hauling furniture

Left Truck stop, Harrisburg, Penn. Two KWs and one Peterbilt all very chromed and clean. The KW on the right has a deflector shield to persuade bugs not to hit the windshield. The Big Arch Leasing of Alabama Inc. truck is typical of the US trucking industry *Right* Concave, convex, flat and full vision on Route 15, Las Vegas. There's a CB aerial there too

International Harvester carrying
cardboard at San Jose on Highway
101 out of San Francisco. Old but
strong

El Centro in the desert in California
– a motel truckstop diner in the early
evening

Top Freightliner cabover with rented box van trailer. Very straight and unglamorous *Bottom* Hand lined custom paintwork features on many rigs, even those which are part of one company. The painter could have as many as fifty or more rigs to work on repeating the same insignia on each

Cattle rig or bull hauler – Pete
conventional at El Centro in the
sunset

DUSK TO DAWN

Left Skeeter Boats of Kilgore, Texas – GMC cabover hauling a yacht trailer. The whole rig was a miriad of running lights emphasised by those on the front *Above* This Aerodyne equipped Kenworth double sleeper cabover is like a mini hotel inside. The driver should lack nothing in home comforts. The rig has pulled into a gas station in Springfield, Ohio

Left Just out of Chula Vista north of the
Mexican border in Southern California
this White Freightliner speeds through
the early morning. See how it tends to
rear-up slightly at the front *Right* Going
south this time in the early evening out
of Santa Barbara on Route 101. That's
the ocean in the background and the
night ahead

Below Over 90 mph – Chula Vista near San Diego *Bottom* Midnight but always open – Williams, and maybe home for this tar truck *Right* Perhaps the busiest trucking centre in mid Southern California is here at Bakersfield. There were 200 trucks and no cars at this truckstop which provides a cross-roads for the industry

Alabama Blue Jay is a highly customised Peterbilt conventional. Although it looked beautiful it smelled appalling because of its onion load. The night heat created the problem

Left The same onion truck on the previous spread but this time with its running lights lit *Right* International fuel tanker capable of dropping its 8750 US gallon load in thirty minutes. Trucker Don Church would make six drops per night in the Chula Vista, San Diego area

The arch of the exhaust smoke pouring out of the stack indicates nothing but high speed for this Freightliner out of Chula Vista. The one street light belies the grim area that this is

CONVENTIONAL

Custom Peterbilt conventional with 350 Cummins engine and 13-speed transmission – some $16,000 was spent on customizing alone. This rig hauls sand during the building of a flood control system at Lakeside, San Diego *Above* Kingsize sleeper KW rig at Glendale, Los Angeles. 'Elf Serve' is really self-serve!

Above The Fugitive again, this time a side shot showing the mass of chrome and the very cleanliness of the whole rig. The CB aerial shows an illegal booster fitted which could give a range of around 150 miles *Right* Before venturing onto the black top these sand trucks are washed off in a special spray unit. Mirror sunglasses are all part of the cowboy or *Easy Rider* atmosphere

Left, top Plain custom Peterbilt with small sleeper *Bottom left* Hand painted custom symbol with reflected sky in the highly polished panel *Bottom right* A radiator mascot not considered dangerous as it might on a car *Below* Old trucks of this medium size are rare although GMCs of this age are not generally so rare. This classic was photographed on the coast road, Route 1, between Los Angeles and San Francisco

Ford sand truck, this time with its special belly dump trailer in full view. This conventional is not customized although it does have an air conditioner

Above Mack and aerofoil out of Williams. Conventional Macks with sleepers are not so common *Left* This Freightliner is anything but standard. This truck was believed built in 1979 and is typical of many showing its numerous licence plates. It was photographed close to the Hoover Dam *Right* Back to the Sunday resting double tankers. Lush vegetation is a feature of much of California

Dave Martin Trucking Co. had leased this rig to the driver who then earns money from each trip he makes. He soon has to make as many trips as possible to maximise it. Hence the 50 to 60 mph being travelled at over the dusty tracks

Bugs everywhere. This Pete rig is resting at
El Centro in the desert after an obviously
long haul *Above* An Autocar in Mahattan
hauling building materials. Even this rig has
been customized with dots on the side! The
indicators on the front bumper are essential
for moving about the New York City streets

CABOVER

Left Almost brand new this KW kingsize sleeper runs
to around $70,000 without the cost of customizing. This
rig is run by a husband and wife team. They come from
Florida but its photographed in San Jose, California
Above Menacing flatbed semi-trailer Freightliner at Gila
Bend

Left Freightliner, Gila Bend
Right Peterbilt, Baker

Cabover Mack in the centre of
Manhattan. An unusual sight
downtown because of its size

Right Three trailers in one. A neat way of ferrying trailers is to turn-tail them like this. This could well be a standard issue Kenworth cabover with double sleeper
Below Bekins Moving & Storage at Gila Bend. *Left* GMC, *right* Ford

Overleaf 'Pray for me, I drive Highway 85'. Peterbilt cabover with double flatbed hauling straw. The truck driver has gone off for home cooking. The rig is on Route 5 outside Los Banos

Manufactured by White, the Western
Star is a rare truck. This is a standard
cab with usual paint. Once again this
was photographed in Los Banos

Sleeper rig and 'dozer near Tijuana. The load, of
course, is scruffy and so is the immediate
environment but the truck is yet again immaculate

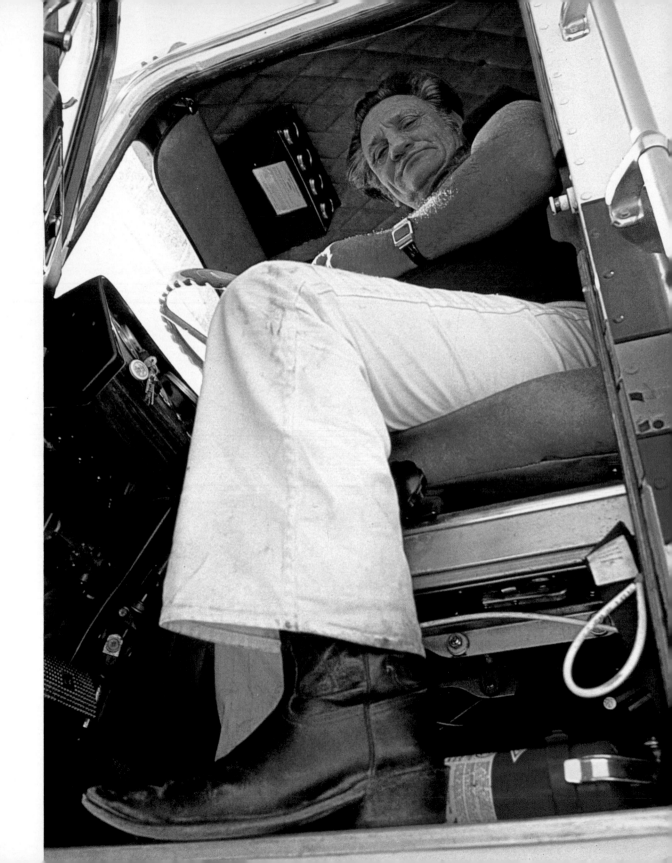

TRUCKER

Left Jay Hamilton's trouser leg – Jay's White uses a 450 NCT engine with 13-speed Fuller transmission to haul his forty-two feet cold box loaded with beef from Denver to California. Coffee, but not pills, keeps him awake
Above Eric Felder is the second driver for this Cummins 400 White stopped at a 76 truck stop west of Las Vegas. He helps to haul vegetables up to 4000 miles per week

Freightliner cabover – rev counter, speedo, CB, coffee flask, power operated factory extra seats, stereo and air conditioner – flight deck

Above Dug Bryant, black trucker out of Phoenix driving a White. He works
a fourteen hour day and has done so for twenty-two years as an owner/
operator. His $2000 per week turnover has to pay all costs
Right Barry Brotnow has been driving for fifty years. He's working out his
route in his Cat engined Peterbilt. He spends four days per month at home
while working his Western Electric haulage contract out of Phoenix
Overleaf Bud Blanset hauls for Dixey Line. His Freightliner runs a 430
Detroit engine and a 9 speed Fuller. He thinks that his custom leather
interior trim is the thing to have for his 2000 miles per week

Vons supermarket chain – the West's
Finest – often run double trailers. Their
drivers have just re-started after a Sunday
morning break

Custom roof, this time inside *The Fugitive*

ALLIED VAN LINES
BROADVIEW, ILLINOIS
ICC MC 15735

Left Little lady – there are an increasing number of husband and wife teams, and this means that the wife must drive. Here she's learning *Above* 1975 Peterbilt, 350 Cummins, 13-speed RTO 125/3 transmission. The driver remains guarded by his sunglasses *Overleaf* International Coors beer truck. Jake McCaulay starts at 5.30 am and finishes at 6.00 pm five days a week making local deliveries around Glendale, Arizona. His International runs a Cummins 235 and 10-speed Roadranger

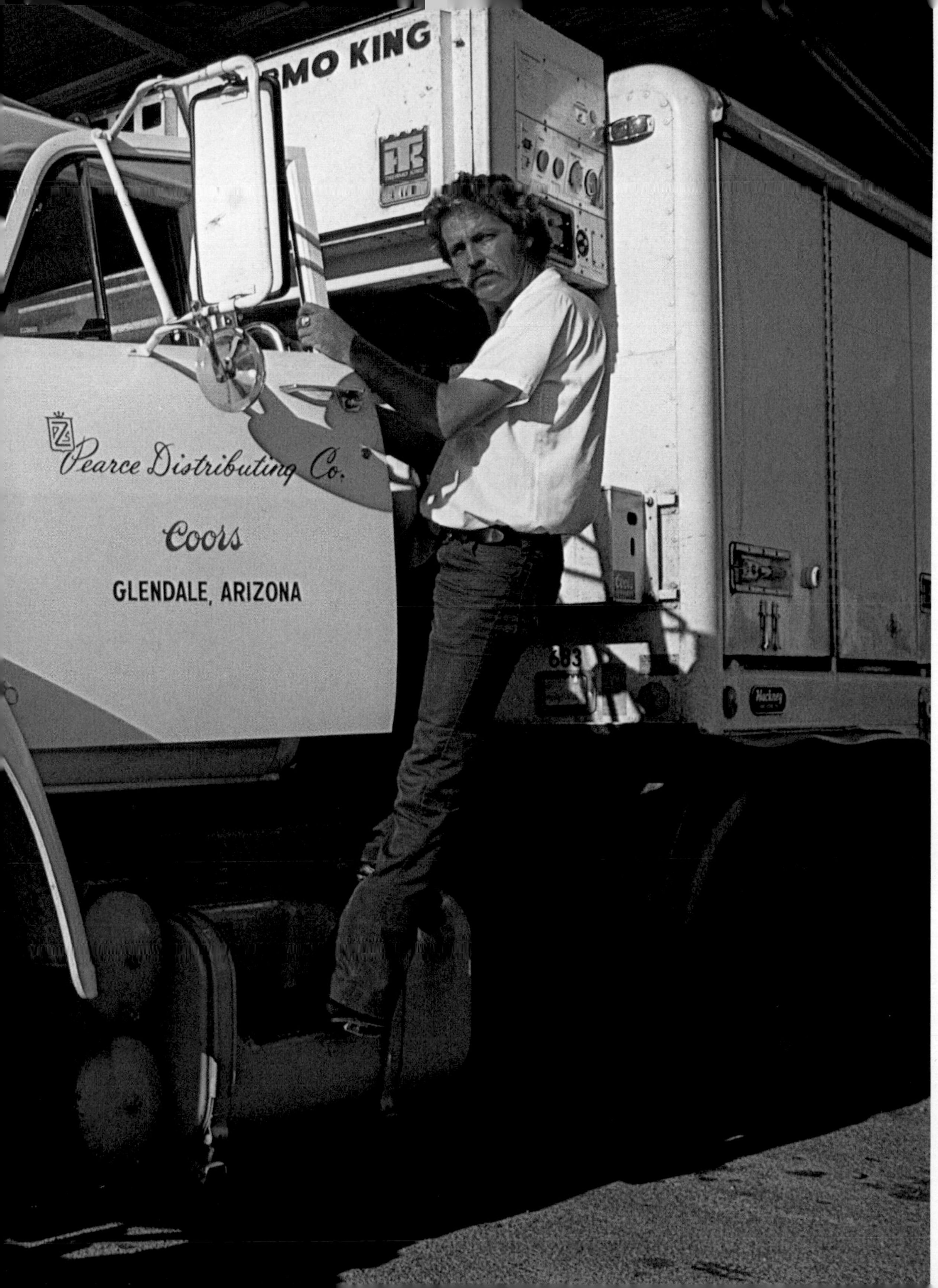
MO KING
Pearce Distributing Co.
Coors
GLENDALE, ARIZONA
683

WRECKER

Above Rightoff! *Left* 'The Happy Hooker'
is an early Mack wrecker in Las Vegas.
There's no question that he is 'Number 1'

Piggyback – all reconditioned
Peterbilts – outside a Ventura
wrecker's yard

East Coast customizing using paint and metalflake. There are many people now performing this type of sign writing and painting as a profession

SMOKEY AND SMOKE

Left Chuck Brown, Senior Police Officer,
Oceanside, California. .375 Magnum and
Kawasaki KZ1000 Police (motorcycle)
Above Lynn Ideus, Officer, Sunset Point
(ninety miles south of Flagstaff) runs this
Plymouth Police mostly to check the speed
of speeding truckers. His biggest enemy is
the Fuzzbuster

Chuck Brown chasing. He says his Kawasaki will run 120 mph. Whatever he says it will be faster than the Harley it replaced

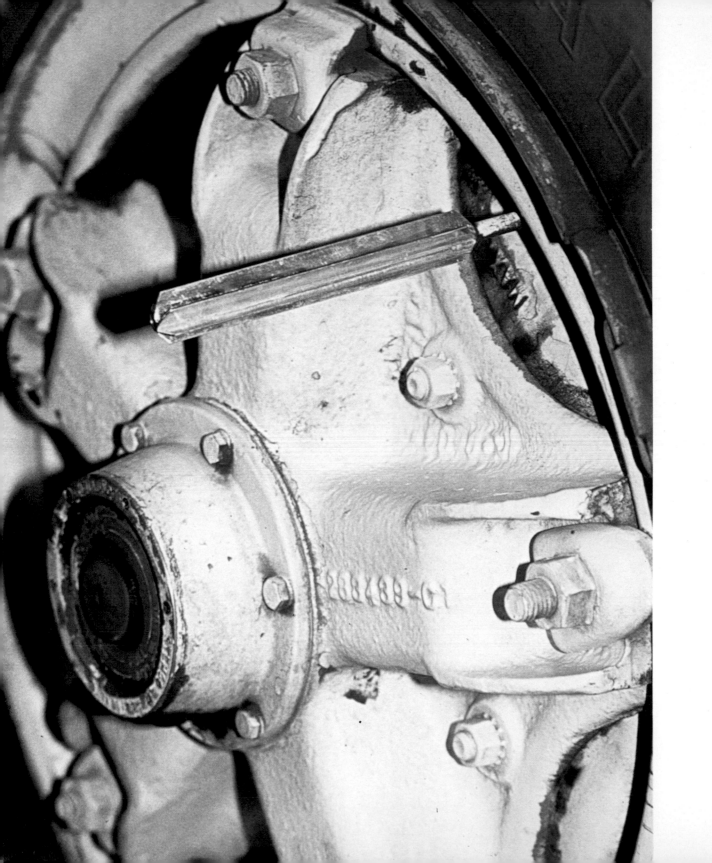

Left This is the standard radar speed trap
scrambler which many trucks have fitted to their
front wheels. It is openly sold in truck stops
Above The badge (and pens)

Pirsch fire truck of the San Clemente
Fire Department was built in 1957
but still runs well. It is one of four
with eighty-five foot ladders in that
department. Pirsch specialize in the
manufacture of fire trucks

Above Closeup of the emblem. The mascot is the red
light! *Right* Downtown San Francisco. A Le France
fire truck speeds on its way to a fire (or earthquake).
This was shot from the 27th floor with a 28 mm wide
angle lens